TREES AT LEISURE

BY

ANNA BOTSFORD COMSTOCK

THIS EDITION PUBLISHED 2021

BY HEARTHROOM PRESS

ILLUSTRATIONS BY: S R BADMIN

ORIGINAL WORK PUBLISHED IN 1916

BY

COMSTOCK PUBLISHING COMPANY

A SPECIAL THANKS TO

PROFESSOR RALPH W. CURTIS

HARRY H. KNIGHT

LEWIS B. HENDERSHOT

VERNE MORTON

FOR MORE INFORMATION, CONTACT:
HEARTHROOM PRESS
INFO@HEARTHROOMPRESS.COM

TREES AT LEISURE

While resting there, his eyes raised to the overhanging branches, there may well have come to him an uplift into the vague consciousness of a realm of beauty as far above his ken as the branches and shifting leaves were above the reach of his hand.

4

If we could know the part that trees have played in the aesthetic education of man, mayhap we should find that they began this great and silent schooling when the native boy, weary from his chase in the hot sun, sought refuge in their refreshing shade. While resting there, his eyes raised to the overhanging branches, there may well have come to him an uplift into the vague consciousness of a realm of beauty as far above his ken as the branches and shifting leaves were above the reach of his hand. Ages may have passed before man gained sufficient mental stature to pay admiring tribute to the tree standing in all the glory of its full leafage, shimmering in the sunlight, making its myriad bows to the restless winds; but eons must have lapsed before the human eye grew keen enough and the human soul large enough to give sympathetic comprehension to the beauty of bare branches laced across changing skies, which is the tree-lover's full heritage.

However, it is during this winter resting time that the tree stands revealed to the uttermost, ready to give its most intimate confidences to those who love it.

6

The mortal who has never enjoyed a speaking acquaintance with some individual tree is to be pitied; for such an acquaintance, once established, naturally ripens into a friendliness that brings serene comfort to the human heart, whatever the heart of the tree may or may not experience. To those who know them, the trees, like other friends, seem to have their periods of reaching out for sympathetic understanding. How often this outreaching is met with repulse will never be told; for tree friends never reproach us, but wait with calm patience for us to grow into comprehension.

In winter, we are prone to regard our trees as cold, bare, and dreary; and we bid them wait until they are again clothed in verdure before we may accord to them comradeship. However, it is during this winter resting time that the tree stands revealed to the uttermost, ready to give its most intimate confidences to those who love it. It is indeed a superficial acquaintance that depends upon the garb worn for half the year ; and to those who know them, the trees display even more individuality in the winter than in the summer. The summer is the tree's period of reticence, when, behind its mysterious veil of green, it is so busy with its own life processes that it has no time for confidences, and may only now and then fling us a friendly greeting.

At no other time of year is the American elm more beautiful than when it traces its graceful lines against snow and gray.

The recognition of trees in the season of winter is a matter of experience and may not be learned from a book. Often the differences that distinguish them are too subtle to be put into words. However, some species portray their individuality in such a graphic manner that the wayfarer, though a fool, need not err therein. Such is the elm that graces our meadows and fields, where it marks the sites of fences present and past. At no other time of year is the American elm more beautiful than when it traces its flowing lines against snow and gray skies. Whether the tree be young, slender, and svelte or grown to full stature, whether it be vase- or fountain-shaped, there is in its dark twig-fringed bole a grace shown in upward expansion, which is continued in the uplift of spreading branches and finds perfect expression in the final twigs that droop as if in loving memory of their summer burden of leaves, in token of which the oriole's nest is tenderly held in safe keeping.

In sharp contrast to the benignant, inviting curves of the elm are the self-centered outlines of the isolated sugar maples.

In sharp contrast to the benignant and inviting curves of the elm is the self-centered outline of the isolated sugar maple. Even this tree is more graceful in winter than in summer. It displays its many straight branches, lifted skyward and ending in finely-divided but well-ordered sprays; while earlier, it was merely an elongated green period that served to punctuate the summer landscape. Widely different in habit is the great maple of the woodland, whose noble bole rises, a living pillar, to the arches that uphold the forest canopy. We do not need to look up to its high branches to know it; for its shining gray color and a certain majesty of mien proclaim at once its identity and its place as a peer in the forest realm.

Who would believe that a granite-gray column could hold a store of sweetness!

Who would believe that a granite-gray column could hold store of sweetness which a few weeks later we may have for the asking! The maple, more than other trees, seems to need to have its close fisted bushiness pruned away by jealous neighbors to make it great and fine and generous. To those who think that in winter a maple is simply a maple we should like to point out in contrast to the tree just mentioned, the graceful, smooth, gray-barked red maple, that, true to its name keeps its bit of winter landscape warm with its glow, each of its bud-laden twigs a ruddy dreamer of scarlet past and crimson future.

But, to return to the field, there are other tree tenants of the safe fence corners that are worth knowing: the low broad thorn-apple, with its more or less horizontal branches dividing and subdividing into a frenzy of twiglets, shows a fitting framework for the great bridal bouquet which will cover it next June; the straight-limbed bird cherry with its shining bark, perhaps in ragged transverse rolls; and those shrub cousins of the trees, the sumacs, like bronze candelabra, holding their dark pinacles aloft, black sockets whence once blazed crimson flame.

Many of the trees planted by man for man's enjoyment give as good returns in winter as in summer

Many of the trees planted by man for man's enjoyment give as good returns in winter as in summer: the honey locust rearing its slender height protectingly above the homestead, or above the memory of one, its great twisted branches making picturesque any scene, however homely, its maze of twigs still holding its large spirally rolled pods, which will in due time skate away over icy snowdrifts and plant their seeds far from the parent tree; the black locust, less picturesque, seemingly conscious of its nakedness, retaining a scanty garment of little rustling pods, until spring shall again bring to it its exquisitely wrought leaf mantle; the horse chestnut, painting itself in broad style against the pearly sky, its sparse, bud-tipped, clumsy twigs appearing like knobbed antennas put forth to test the safety of the neighborhood; the tall, straight, cut-leaved birch with its central column of white, and white branches ascending stark and stiff and then suddenly breaking into dark fountains of deliquescence ; the Lombardy poplar, a spire of green against summer horizons, now a vague wraith through whose transparent form we can see the sky and landscape beyond; and, as picturesque as any, the old apple tree, its great angularly twisted branches bearing a forest of aspiring shoots.

15

The willows, unwilling even in summer to be taken for other tree species, assert their peculiarities quite as vigorously in winter.

The stream borders give us trees of strong individuality. The willows, unwilling even in summer to be taken for other tree species, assert their peculiarities quite as vigorously in winter. The golden osier displays its magnificent trunk and giant limbs upholding a mass of terminal shoots that tinge with warm ocher the winter landscape. The black willow, having cast its sickle leaves to the autumn winds, lifts itself in twins or triplets, or even larger families of sister trees, that stand in close confab on borders of murmuring streams; while the little pussy willows gather in neighborly groups close to living brooks, where in summer they shade the darting minnows and in winter cuddle contentedly under their snow blanket and listen to the contented gurgling of the ice-bound waters.

How different the young trees, so slender and shapely, and overfond of reflecting their graceful figures in the still pools of streams!

The sycamore loses nothing of its effectiveness when it loses its foliage. The dull yellow of the trunk and the pale gray of the great undulating, serpent-like branches, blotched with white, show as distinctly against the snow as they did against the summer green; the very smoothness of the few large limbs makes us unprepared for the way they break up into a madness of terminal branchlets, to which still cling here and there a button-ball not yet whipped off its fibrous string. How different the young trees, so slender and shapely, and overfond of reflecting their graceful figures in the still pools of streams! It might seem that the stream guards wear a uniform of khaki, in evidence of which behold the slender bole of the great-toothed poplar and that of the quaking aspen which has shaken off its agitation with its leaves, meets the winter winds with serene courage; and likewise clad is the cottonwood, that guardian of western rivers, on which, though it be ragged and unkempt, the traveler's eye lingers lovingly.

They now flaunt their scant, jaundiced spires against the blue sky,
unconscious of the sad picture they make in their coniferally unnatural
nakedness.

20

Another water-loving tree, which revels in swamps, is the pepperidge; extravagant in horizontal branches and twigs when young, it stands gaunt and bare when old, its main trunk looking like a decrepit mast with a few dilapidated yardarms hanging to it. The tamaracks are its neighbors; in summer graceful lacy cones, they now flaunt their scant, jaundiced spires against the blue sky, unconscious of the sad picture they make in their coniferally unnatural nakedness.

21

In the forest depths in winter, we trust more to the shape and color of the bole and to the texture of the bark than to the branches above for recognition of old acquaintances.

In the forest depths in winter, we trust more to the shape and color of the bole and to the texture of the bark than to the branches above for recognition of old acquaintances. The beech wears the crest of its nobility woven into the hues of its firm, smooth bark; its lower branches retain all winter many of their leaves, russet now and sere, whispering lonesomely to the winds; and with its leaves it retains its burrs, empty now of nuts and hanging in constellations, quenched and black against the blue of the zenith. Novices often confuse the trunk of the beech with that of the birch, for the very inadequate reason that both may be transversely striped with white. The beech's stripes are woven into the texture of the firm fine grained bark and are as unlike those of the tatterdemalion birch as could well be imagined. The white birch coquettes with us with her untidy silken ribbons from the forest depths in a manner which a self-respecting beech would scorn; and she is not the only one of her kind that wears shining ribbons, although we are less likely to notice the darker colors of the black and yellow birches.

...learn to greet each as a friend well known and well beloved!

In all the woodland there is no more beautiful bark to be found than that which pencils the trunk of the white ash in fine vertical lines and fades away into smoothness on the lower limbs. The ash branchlets, though of pleasing lines, are few and coarse; those of white ash give the effect of being warped into terminal curves. Contrast the bark of the white ash with the rugged virile bark of the hemlock and then turn to the basswood's straight bole and note the fine elongated network which covers it and learn to greet each as a friend well known and well beloved!

The hornbeam, or blue beech, ever tries to tie into a knot its twisted slender branches; often even the grain of the wood is hard twisted, so that the close bark shows as a loose spiral. One wonders if it is because of this vital writhing that the sap which slowly oozes from the tree in spring soon turns red as blood. Very different in appearance is her sister, the hop hornbeam, whose slender trunk I covered with narrow flattened scales that flake off untidily.

The oak cannot be spared from the winter landscape.

The oak cannot be spared from the winter landscape. It is only when the oak stands bared like a runner for a race that we realize wherein its supremacy lies. We have made it a synonym of staunchness and sturdiness, but not until we see naked the massive trunk and the strong limbs bent and gnarled for thrusting back the blasts, can we understand why the oak is staunch. However, there are oaks and oaks, and each one fights time and tempest in its own peculiar armor and in its own brave way. The red, the scarlet, and the black oaks show a certain ruggedness as of knotted sinews in their boles, and their dark gray bark, irregularly furrowed, changes into flat planes above and smooths out into a soft, dark gray covering on the vigorous though twisted upper branches. The bark of the white oak is pale gray, divided by shallow fissures into elongated scales, yet withal a dignified dress for a noble tree. To one who is fortunate enough to have had a Quaker grandfather, the white oak will bring a vision of him arrayed in his First Day garb. However, there are vast differences in the white oaks of America, as we keenly realize if we compare the conservative white oak of the East with its erratic picturesque sister of the Pacific Coast, "picturesqueness gone mad," as described by an artist trying to sketch.

grace is gained as strength is lost.

The hickories resemble the oaks except that they are more refined and less virile; their limbs are shorter and grace is gained as strength is lost. Each species asserts an unmistakable individuality. The shagbark vaunts the superfluity of its raiment; the pignut lifts a narrow oblong head, its lower branches gnarled and drooping; less drooping are the lower branches of the mockernut and much more rounded its outline, while the bitternut bole divides into several large branches that spread and form a broad head. Those cousins of the hickories, the black walnut and the butternut, attract our attention by their sparse rather coarse terminal twigs. The wide flattened ridges of its deeply furrowed bark distinguish the butternut and often suggest the long smooth slats that hold the chestnut bole in tight embrace.

Brave tree folk are these conifers of ours, whether their span of life extends over three centuries, like our pines, or twenty, like the redwoods.

No winter scene is perfect without the evergreens; although these, until dead, never display to our curious eyes the history of their struggles for life, as written on their naked branches; yet to them alone among trees has a voice been given. The poet has often been a more sensitive listener than seer in the natural world, and from the earliest times he has resung for his fellow-men the mysterious song of the Although our evergreens retain their working garb, yet they are trees of fine leisure during the months of frost and ice; and whether they lift their mighty heads singly above the forest level or group themselves in green-black masses, they make strong the composition of the winter picture. Nothing brings out the perspective of the snow-covered hills like a clump of great hemlocks in the foreground; and the tassels of the pine are never so beautiful as when tossed in defiance against the stormy winter sky. Brave tree folk are these conifers of ours, whether their span of life extends over three centuries, like our pines, or twenty, like the redwoods. They give us a wide sense of the earth as an abiding-place.

Such a day is the apotheosis of winter, and one must needs go into the still forest and worship.

On some winter mornings even the most careless of mortals must pay admiring tribute to the trees, for again are they clad, this time in a glittering raiment of soft snow. Such a day is the apotheosis of winter, and one must needs go into the still forest and worship. The stillness is commensurate with the whiteness. The trees themselves seem conscious of it, and rebuff the iconoclast breeze with their slowly and silently moving branches. How differently the same forest meets the wind a few days later when a storm is brewing! Then the stiff branches with their twig-sprays tear the howling intruder into whistling shreds, until there is an all-pervading roar that is unlike any other of nature's sounds. It might well be compared to the surf breaking on a rocky shore, if it were not that it seems overwhelming instead of restless, conquering instead of unceasing, sentient instead of unaware.

S·R·Badmin

...now they are painted in warm purple and the same royal color is to be seen in the shadows of the snowy valleys...

February is of the winter months the impressionist, the colorist. In December the forest masses on the hills were brown or gray; now they are painted in warm purple and the same royal color is to be seen in the shadows of the snowy valleys through a veil of sapphire haze that brings sky and forest and white hills into restful unity. This slowly increasing richness of color of the late winter in our northern landscapes is not often appreciated. Long before the frost leaves the ground and the snow slinks away from the hill-sides, the impulse of the warming sun is caught in bark and buds. It is this warm tint of the forest in February that brings to the heart the first subtle prescience of spring, even before the chickadee feels it and makes the still woods echo with his sweet prophesying "phoebe" song.

Happy is he who keeps his picture gallery always with him ; his life is full of joy!

Happy is he who keeps his picture gallery always with him ; his life is full of joy! To each of us is given a sky which many times a day is painted anew for our delectation; and it is never more perfect than when in winter it is a background against which the trees are etched. Whether the horizon be crimson with the sunrise, or gold with the sunset; whether it displays the blue of the turquoise uplifted into the color of the rose on snowy mornings, or glows with the amethystine splendor of afternoons or the beryl tints of evening; the bare branches strongly outlined against it in harmonious contrast complete the color chord; with infinitely varying hues the trees there illuminate, and with exquisite and intricate writing the trees there sign, the diplomas of those whom they have educated.

Made in United States
Orlando, FL
22 December 2021

12262132R00022